SHE SAID IT BEST

Audrey Hepburn

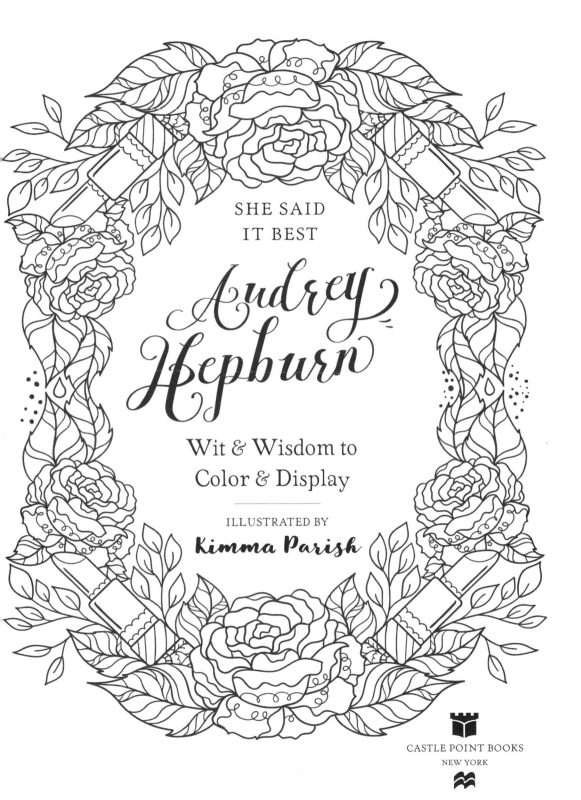

SHE SAID
IT BEST

Audrey Hepburn

Wit & Wisdom to
Color & Display

ILLUSTRATED BY

Kimma Parish

CASTLE POINT BOOKS
NEW YORK

Series design by Katie Jennings Campbell

ISBN 978-1-250-14771-4 (trade paperback)

Our books may be purchased in bulk for promotional, educational, or business use.
Please contact your local bookseller or the
Macmillan Corporate and Premium Sales Department
at 1-800-221-7945, extension 5442, or by e-mail
at MacmillanSpecialMarkets@macmillan.com.

First Edition: October 2017

10 9 8 7 6 5 4 3 2 1

Introduction

AUDREY HEPBURN (May 4, 1929 – January 20, 1993) reigns as the emblem of fashion, symbol of grace, and the model of generosity to rule them all. As one of the most admired actresses to come up in the Golden Age of Hollywood, Audrey brought elegance, effervescence, and doe-eyed charm to the stage and screen. From her very first leading role in *Roman Holiday* (1953) and her comic portrayal in *Funny Face* (1957), to her irreplaceable presence in *Breakfast at Tiffany's* (1961), Audrey stole the hearts of cinema-goers and style mavens alike.

Audrey's prolific film and theatre pursuits were complemented by her incomparable sense of style. Her bond with fashion designer Hubert de Givenchy was an enduring friendship and camaraderie of style that could be seen on and off screen. This legendary actress is also remembered as a dedicated humanitarian. She was a UNICEF International Goodwill Ambassador, and she was awarded the Presidential Medal of Freedom for her efforts to children in need. Audrey's poise and wisdom can be found in the many interviews and speeches she gave during her career and philanthropic efforts. Within the pages of *She Said It Best: Audrey Hepburn*, you'll find lovely, hand-drawn illustrations paying homage to her legacy, accompanied by little bits of wisdom on love and fashion, and insights on giving and kindness.

SHE SAID IT BEST is a celebration of the women who have shown us life in vibrant color. From famous authors and musicians to philanthropists and socialites, these women are the voices of many generations, each of whom has written, spoken, or sung wisdom into our lives. Whether it's mending a broken heart, standing up for a cause, or adding some class—and maybe some sass—to any situation, the advice and witticisms from these beloved women continue to inspire, encourage, and empower.

This unique coloring book series captures the insight, beauty, and timelessness of these leading women—from Dolly Parton to Jacqueline Kennedy Onassis—with some of their most memorable and distinguished words. Hand-drawn illustrations adorn each saying and convey the unique charm and spirit that made them extraordinary. Decorate the pages of *She Said It Best* in honor of the woman on the cover, or to fill your world with a little more love, light, and wisdom.

People, even more than things, have
to be restored, renewed, revived, reclaimed,
and redeemed; never throw out anyone.

Success is like reaching an important birthday and finding you're exactly the same.

I was born
with an enormous need for
affection, and a terrible need to give it.

Giving is living.

You can tell more about a person by
what he says about others than you can
by what others say about him.

...I think that's what life is all about,
actually, about children and flowers.

We all want to be loved, don't we?
Everyone looks for a way of finding love. It's a
constant search for affection in every walk of life.

Forgive quickly.
Kiss slowly.
Love truly.
Laugh uncontrollably
and never regret
anything that
made you smile.

The past, I think, has helped me appreciate the present—
and I don't want to spoil any of it by fretting about the future.

I decided, very early on, just to accept life unconditionally;
I never expected it to do anything special for me, yet I
seemed to accomplish far more than I had ever hoped.

If you stop wanting to give,
there's nothing more to live for.

I'm half-Irish, half-Dutch, and I was born in
Belgium. If I was a dog, I'd be in a hell of a mess!

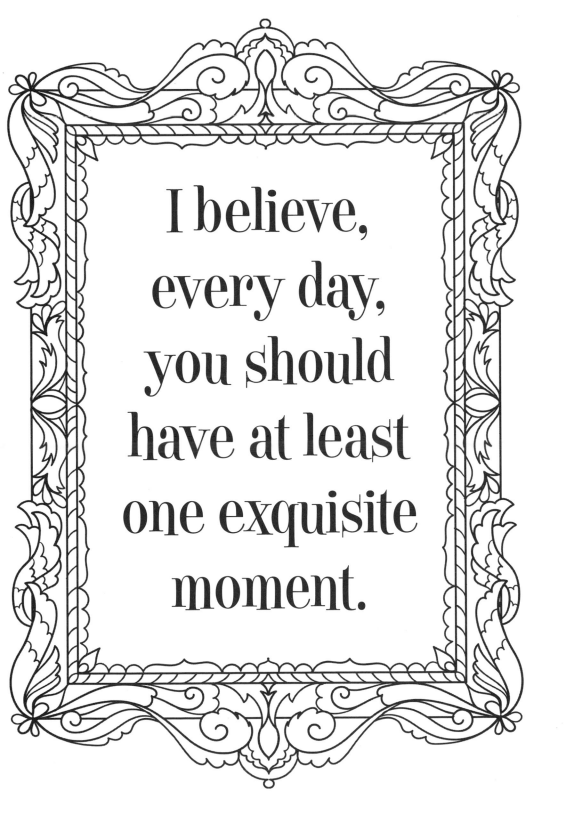

I believe,
every day,
you should
have at least
one exquisite
moment.

For beautiful eyes, look for the good
in others; for beautiful lips, speak only
words of kindness; and for poise, walk with
the knowledge that you are never alone.

The beauty of a woman is seen in her eyes, because that is the doorway to her heart, the place where love resides.

There is one difference between a long life and a
great dinner; in the dinner, the sweet things come last.

OPPORTUNITIES DON'T OFTEN
COME ALONG. SO, WHEN THEY DO,
YOU HAVE TO GRAB THEM.

I have learnt how to live...how to be in the world
and of the world, and not just to stand aside and watch.

I BELIEVE
THAT TOMORROW
IS ANOTHER DAY
AND I BELIEVE
IN MIRACLES.

Living is like tearing through a museum.
Not until later do you really start absorbing what
you saw, thinking about it, looking it up in a book, and
remembering—because you can't take it in all at once.

For me the only things of interest
are those linked to the heart.

If my world were to cave in tomorrow, I would look back on all the pleasures, excitements and worthwhilenesses I have been lucky enough to have had.

It is too much to hope that I shall keep up my success.
I don't ask for that. All I shall do is my best—and hope.

For my whole life, my favorite activity was reading.
It's not the most social pastime.

I may not always be offered work,
but I'll always have my family.

I've had my share of difficult moments,
but whatever difficulties I've gone through,
I've always gotten the prize at the end.

I don't need a bedroom to prove my womanliness.
I can convey just as much sex appeal,
picking apples off a tree or standing in the rain.

I tried always to do better, saw always
a little further. I tried to stretch myself.

*Some people dream of
having a big swimming pool.
With me, it's closets.*

I believe in being strong when
everything seems to be going wrong.

Let's face it, a nice creamy chocolate cake does
a lot for a lot of people; it does for me.

The most important thing is to enjoy your life—
to be happy—it's all that matters.

And the beauty of a woman, with passing years only grows!

I believe that happy girls
are the prettiest girls.

They say love is the best investment;
the more you give, the more you get in return.

PICK THE DAY.
ENJOY IT—TO THE HILT.

When you have nobody you
can make a cup of tea for,
when nobody needs you,
that's when I think life is over.

True friends are families which you can select.

Good things aren't supposed to just fall into your lap.
God is very generous, but He expects you to do your part first.

...remember you have another hand: the first is to help yourself, the second is to help others.

You have to be absolutely frank with yourself. Face your handicaps, don't try to hide them. Instead, develop something else.

A quality education has the power to transform societies in a single generation...

I don't take my life seriously, but I
do take what I do—in my life—seriously.

If I'm honest, I have to tell you I still read
fairy tales, and I like them best of all.

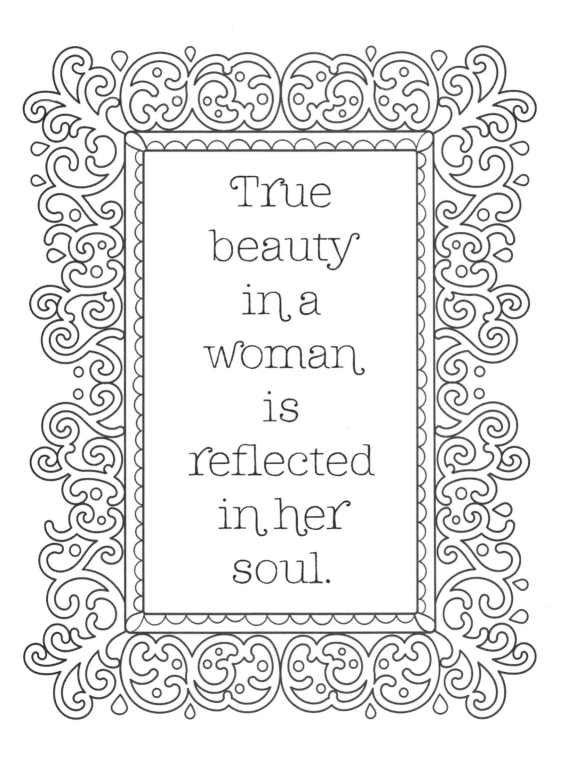

True
beauty
in a
woman
is
reflected
in her
soul.

Make-up can only make you look pretty
on the outside but it doesn't help if you're ugly
on the inside. Unless you eat the make-up.

Nothing is impossible,
the word itself says "I'm possible"!

...I love to be alone. It doesn't bother me one bit. I'm my own company.

Why change? Everyone has his own style. When you have found it, you should stick to it.

Your heart just breaks, that's all. But you can't judge, or point fingers. You just have to be lucky enough to find someone who appreciates you.

I believe in kissing, a lot.

I love people who make me laugh.
I honestly think it's the thing
I like most, to laugh.

THERE
IS A SHADE
OF RED
FOR EVERY
WOMAN.